# William F. Keys
## of Joshua Tree National Park

*Imagine his legacy.*

*Norma Ardoetena*

**Books by Thomas Crochetiere:**

**The JTNP series;**

The History of Joshua Tree National Park –
History [2019; *Fifth Edition, 10/2023*]

Keys Desert Queen Ranch: A Visual & Historical Tour –
History [2020; *Second Edition, 4/2021*]

The Trail Guide to Joshua Tree National Park –
Hiking/History [2022; *Second Edition, 3/2023*]

William F. Keys of Joshua Tree National Park –
a Biography [2023]

**Also by Thomas Crochetiere;**

Remembering my Miss Vicki – a Biography [2011]

Our Life Well-Lived – a Memoir [2012]

America's National Parks At a Glance – Travel [2016]

Gateway to the Morongo Basin – History [2021]

A Treasure of Fine Words –
Literature/Book of Quotations [2022]


Cover photo of Bill, circa 1955; NPS photo
Back photo of Thomas; JTNPA/Desert Institute

# William F. Keys

## of Joshua Tree National Park

Joshua Tree
National
Park

By
Thomas Crochetiere

tcrochetiere@outlook.com


ISBN: 979-8-88955-297-0


Printed in the United States of America


Published in cooperation with:
JOSHUA TREE NATIONAL PARK ASSOCIATION
74485 National Park Drive
Twentynine Palms, California 92277
www.joshuatree.org

(also available in eBook format)

# Table of Contents

"If history were taught in the form of stories, it would never be forgotten." -- Rudyard Kipling

# Acknowledgments

Research material from the Joshua Tree National Park Library, including books, reports, studies, and reference materials were used to help create this life story of area pioneer, William Franklin Keys. Information found on NPS.gov and thelandpatents.com were also used. I would like to credit and thank the following resources for their contributions to the writing of this book. Writings by Willis Keys, Art Kidwell, and Jeff Ohlfs were used to verify and confirm some of the history of Bill Keys.

We will be forever grateful to the Keys family and heirs for their continued support as we share the family history and keep the memories alive through this and every publication about Bill Keys and the Desert Queen Ranch.

Bill Keys is just one of many pioneers who would make their home in what we know today as Joshua Tree National Park. Arriving in 1910, Bill had free rein in the area. When Joshua Tree National Monument was established in 1936, this new monument completely encircled his ranch and mining claims. Although his relationship with the National Park Service was strained at first, he would go on to become a part of the park's history.

Joshua Tree National Park acknowledges the Maara'yam (Serrano), Nüwü (Chemehuevi), Kawiya (Cahuilla), and Aha Macav (Mohave) peoples as the original stewards of the land on which the park now sits. Joshua Tree National Park preserves the scenic, natural, and cultural resources representative of the Mojave and Colorado Deserts' rich biological and geological diversity, cultural history, wilderness, recreational values, and outstanding opportunities for education and scientific study. As stewards of Joshua Tree National Park's natural and cultural resources, today's park managers and Indigenous people recognize the importance of developing a comprehensive approach to resource management.

# Acts of Congress Cited in this Book

When a bill is passed in identical form by both the Senate and the House, it is sent to the President for signature. If the President signs the bill, it becomes a law. Laws are also known as Acts of Congress.

**Homestead Act of 1862**: To encourage westward migration, Congress passed the Homestead Act of 1862, which provided up to 160 acres of federal land to anyone who lived on it or improved it, for five years.

**Forest Reserve Act of 1891**: Authorized the President of the United States to designate public lands in the west into what were then called "forest reserves." The law gave the President the authority to unilaterally set aside forest reserves from land in the public domain. The act subsided by 1910.

**Antiquities Act of 1906**: The Antiquities Act was the first U.S. law to provide general legal protection of cultural and natural resources of historic or scientific interest on federal lands. President Theodore Roosevelt signed the Antiquities Act on June 8, 1906.

**Taylor Grazing Act of 1934**: Congress passed the Taylor Grazing Act of 1934 (named after Rep. Edward Taylor of Colorado), which led to the creation of grazing districts. In these districts, grazing use was apportioned and regulated.

# Introduction

This is the story of William F. Keys. Born and raised in rural Nebraska, he left school while in the 5<sup>th</sup> grade to work in his father's shoemaking shop. An avid reader, Bill often imagined himself living a very different life and partaking in many adventures. After a strained relationship with his father, Bill decided to strike out on his own.

Throughout Bill's long journey, he made his way to California. Having become a cowboy along the way, Bill learned the many skills he would need to make a life for himself and his eventual family. He was self-reliant and adamantly protected the needs and interests of his family. Bill led a life like no other and became a success story when all the odds were against him.

Every effort was made to verify the accuracy of Bill Keys' history. However, the author found some conflicting statements as to what happened when. What you are about to read is true, to the best of my knowledge, after countless hours of research and verification. The intent of this book is to expose the reader to the inner life of Bill Keys, and in doing so, illuminate his story and allow you to experience his resolve and dreams. So, sit back and relax as you take this journey back in time with Bill Keys, an American pioneer.

William Franklin Keys, late 1950s; NPS photo

# Bill Keys' Story

William F. Keys, or Bill as his friends called him, was born September 27, 1879, in Palisade (Hitchcock County), Nebraska. His name at birth was George Franklin Barth, and he had twelve brothers and sisters. He was the son of John Barth and Margaret Barth, who were German colonists from Russia. The family immigrated to the United States, arriving in Virginia, and eventually settling in Nebraska.

In 1894, at age 15, his horse began to limp. His father told him to put the horse down, but he wanted to seek treatment for his horse instead. Following a heated argument, his father refused to listen to reason. At his father's insistence, he shot the horse. After a long and strained relationship with his father, this was enough for him to realize it was now time to leave home in Culbertson, Nebraska. He soon set out with plans to head west to become a cowboy.

During his first years away, he worked for a while as a ranch hand in Nebraska (possibly in the Sidney area). He then went west to the Colorado Rockies, where he learned to be a miner. He also worked in a mill (ore grinding factory) for a time. He changed his name along the way to Bill Key, presumably after a rancher for whom he had a great deal of respect.

Around 1897/1898, Bill left Colorado and continued to head west. Arriving in Phoenix, Arizona, he found work at a cattle ranch belonging to C.W. Wimmel. Bill soon left the ranch, and along with a friend, Bucky O'Neil, they went to Prescott, Arizona, to join Teddy Roosevelt's Rough Riders. On his enlistment papers, he listed his name as William Franklin Key. During training, Bill's horse fell on him, injuring his spine and preventing him from accompanying the troops to Cuba during the Spanish-American War (April 21, 1898, to August 13, 1898). He soon recovered and moved on.

From Prescott, Bill moved to the town of Jerome, Arizona. In Jerome, he found work at the United Verde Extension Gold, Silver, and Copper Company, in a copper mine and smelter (a factory for smelting a metal from its ore).

In 1900, Bill moved to Needles, California, where he found work as a ranch hand on George Briggs cattle ranch. While there, he befriended several Hualapai Indians, from where he learned much of their ways and language.

In 1901, Bill worked as a ranch hand for the Conrad-Knight Cattle Company near Kingman, Arizona. He took a side job for a time as a deputy sheriff for Mohave County Sheriff Henry Lovin.

When Knight sold his interest in the cattle ranch, Bill hired on at the Gold Roads Mine near Oatman, Arizona. After about a year there, he moved on and began a life as a wandering prospector.

Bill crossed the Colorado River into California and established a small silver mine near Piute Springs in present-day Mojave National Preserve. When that played out, he was hired at the Keystone Mine near Trona, California, in 1903. While working at the Keystone Mine, Bill met Walter Scott, better known as Death Valley Scotty (made famous from the iconic mansion in Death Valley, more commonly known today as Scotty's Castle, which he never owned).

After about a year at the Keystone Mine, Bill went to Soda Lake, California, where he and his friend Matt Amos developed a gold mine called Gold World.

Around 1904, a gold rush was playing out in Goldfield, Nevada, and Bill and Matt could not resist. Finding too many prospectors there, they moved on to Rhyolite, Nevada. Not finding any riches there, Bill left and started prospecting by himself in and around the Funeral Mountains in present-day Death Valley National Park.

After locating several mines in that area, Bill renewed his acquaintance with Walter Scott (Scotty). By this time, Scotty had a wealthy financier to grubstake his mining efforts.

In 1906, Scotty met several investors from New York who wanted to invest in profitable western mines. Scotty was eager to sell them one, but he did not own any at the time. After talking up about a big mine he claimed to own to these prospective investors, Scotty approached Bill and asked if he (Scotty) could show the investors one of Bill's mines. Bill agreed to let Scotty show one of his mines, the Desert Hound.

Scotty then came up with what he thought was a brilliant scheme. Scotty believed he could make more money if he could find a way not to show the investors any mines, but keep the investment they gave him.

Scotty planned to stage a fake holdup of the prospective investors to scare them off from visiting the mine. He could then get other investors to pay him and do the fake holdup again. Scotty passed off Bill as a half-Indian scout, and the two went with Bob Belt (a Panamint Indian) and "Shorty" Smith to stage the ambush. As it turned out, the scheme failed to scare off the eastern investors, so Scotty would now have to show them Bill's mine.

Not letting their first attempt stop them, Scotty tried once again. Scotty, Warner Scott (Scotty's brother), Bill Keys, Jack Brody, and the easterners set off to the mine. Bill and Jack rode ahead to wait in the rocks above Wingate Pass to "ambush" them. Unfortunately, Jack brought a jug of whiskey, and the two consumed it while waiting for Scotty and the easterners to pass by.

It did not help that it was February, and they thought the whiskey would help keep them warm. Needless to say, neither Bill nor Jack was in any condition to pull off their part in the scheme. They were supposed to shoot over the heads of the approaching party but one of the shots hit the leg of Warner instead. Scotty became so angry, he started to ride his horse toward Bill and Jack yelling to stop, that they shot his brother. Suddenly, Bill and Jack hurried down from the rocks and quickly approached Warner, apologizing for shooting him.

The easterners fled without getting any of their investments back. They did, however, report the entire event to the San Bernardino County Sheriff, who swore out warrants for Scotty, Bill, and Jack. After a lengthy search, Bill was located and arrested. The easterners, tired of waiting around for the trial, went back east. With no witnesses, charges were dropped and Bill spent 27 days in jail for his trouble. Bill and Scotty parted ways after that. The event would later be known as the "Battle of Wingate Pass."

Death Valley Scotty, circa 1940s;
courtesy Desert Gazette

Bill sold his claims in the area to a mining company in 1907. He moved to the Los Angeles, California area, where he stayed at Lucky Baldwin's Ranch (an exclusive resort where the wealthy frequent) in Pasadena, California. In the fall of that year, he moved back to Goldfield, Nevada, and would again meet up with Scotty. By this time, Scotty had been hired by Albert Johnson to oversee the construction of the Death Valley Ranch (a so-called "castle"). Scotty, a permanent "guest" at the ranch, told people he owned it, calling it Scotty's Castle. After a while, Bill and Scotty talked it over and agreed to let bygones be bygones. Bill stayed at the castle over the winter, and they remained friends for many years.

In the spring of 1908, Bill went to work at China Ranch near Tecopa Hot Springs, California, but soon set off on another prospecting expedition. After striking it rich from a small claim, Bill took a tour of California and Nevada.

In September 1910, Bill got a job as a cowboy for a cattle outfit at Surprise Spring north of present-day Joshua Tree, California. After hearing gold was found in the area, he set off to try his hand at prospecting north of present-day Twentynine Palms, California. When that did not pan out, Bill got a job as a muleskinner (professional mule driver) for the Desert Queen Mine in present-day Joshua Tree National Park. While working at the Desert Queen Mine, he briefly lived in nearby Twentynine Palms.

Bill worked for an older gentleman by the name of William Morgan. Mr. Morgan soon moved him to his Desert Queen Mill site as the caretaker and to do assay work. It was around this time when Bill met Bill McHaney, who originally built a camp at the mill site in the 1880s and still lived there from time to time. McHaney showed Bill where the Indigenous people used to hunt and gather in the area. He showed him where all the springs were and took him to all the area mining claims and mill sites. This was the beginning of their long friendship.

The Desert Queen Mill was in a box canyon where a year-round spring ran through it. Bill immediately took a liking to the area and after living there for a couple of years, he decided to stay and began to build a permanent cabin to live in. Bill hired his young friend Ray Bolster to help build a grand fireplace and chimney in the cabin. Ray was an exceptional stonemason. They began this project in 1913 and completed it by 1917.

In 1915, Mr. Morgan (a man in his 80s) passed away without paying Bill for a couple of years. Bill soon filed a lien against Morgan's estate for what was owed to him. Bill continued to work on his cabin and live at the mill site. After a two-year court battle with William Morgan's widow (she was 40 years his younger), the Desert Queen Mine and Desert Queen Mill site were deeded over to Bill for back wages in 1917.

Once Bill became the owner of the Desert Queen Mine, he established a homestead claim on it on September 20, 1917, enlarging the property to 80 acres under the Homestead Act of 1862. Bill McHaney abandoned any claim on the camp, and Bill Key established a homestead claim on the Desert Queen Mill site on November 3, 1919.

Included in Bill's 80-acre claim on the mill site was the nearby Cow Camp area, where the Barker and Shay Cattle Company had set up operations around 1905. They built small buildings to stay in and store their gear, as well as a blacksmith shop. This infuriated Will Shay, but Bill's claim was legal.

One of Barker and Shay's men soon visited Bill to keep him busy. While Bill was distracted, they brought in a couple of wagons and took down the cabins and blacksmith shop, taking everything with them. After Bill discovered the theft, he filed a report against Barker and Shay in San Bernardino County court. After a hearing, he was awarded $500.00 in compensation. Unfortunately for Bill, Will Shay's brother, Walter Shay, was the Sheriff of San Bernardino County, and coincidence or not, the court victory for Bill was not recorded, and he never got his money.

Bill enlarged his ranch by establishing a homestead claim for another 320 acres on November 22, 1926. Over time, Bill acquired adjoining lands, enlarging his ranch even more.

Bill Key added "s" to his last name in 1917, due to mail confusion with the Kee family living nearby. Although spelled differently, both names were pronounced the same.

Through Bill's many experiences, he learned everything from nature, to the stars and universe, to animals, farming, and mineralogy. He knew most of the names of the rocks in the area and what minerals were in them by examining them. Just by looking at the formations around, he knew what areas were good for prospecting. Bill was also an accomplished blacksmith and could do almost anything with scrap metal. Over the years, he obtained a vast amount of knowledge about everything he would need to survive, raise a family, and prosper. He also bought a small herd of cattle. Now that his cabin was done and he now legally owned the land around it, Bill decided he needed a wife.

Bill met Frances May Lawton in the Los Angeles area, where she worked as a stenographer and for Western Union Telegraph Company as a telegrapher. Frances was born September 24, 1887, in Ohio; she had three brothers and three sisters. Her family called her Fannie. After dating for a time, they were married on October 8, 1918, in San Bernardino, California; she was 31, and he was 39. Bill took Frances (a city girl) out to what he now called "Desert Queen Ranch," sight unseen, in his 1915 Model T Roadster. She immediately fell in love with the ranch.

Muriel and Constance (Frances' sisters),
Frances and Bill Keys, circa 1918; NPS photo

Altogether, Frances and Bill had seven children. William Jr. was born in September 1919, but sadly he died five days after birth. In January 1921, their second child was born, and they named him Willis. Their first daughter, Ellen "Virginia," was born in January 1923, and then another son, David, was born in August 1924, but he also died five days after birth. In August 1926, Ellsworth was born, then Patricia in October 1928, and finally Phyllis in October 1931. After the death of William Jr., Bill set aside one acre of the ranch land for a family cemetery. William Jr. and David were both buried there. He carved headstones for each of them. Bill placed the cemetery away from the ranch. He put it close enough for Frances to take a hike to go visit, and far enough away to be out of sight, and out of mind if she needed.

Ellsworth, Virginia, Willis, and Patricia,
circa 1933; NPS photo

In 1921, Bill and Frances constructed what they called the Cow Camp Reservoir. They used this to catch and store rainwater for irrigation and for their cattle herds. The dam is located near their ranch, above Cow Camp.

Bill leased the Desert Queen Mine to DeFaus Geil of Morongo Valley, California in 1923. Geil worked it for about one month and purportedly pocketed $25,000 in gold before giving up the lease and returning to Morongo Valley. He then used the money to build the Morongo Valley Inn.

Desert Queen Mine, circa 2015

Frances' mother (Lena Lawton) visited often, staying in the second-story room of the cabin. Bill built a guest cabin for when Frances' brothers came to visit. They called this the "north house." The cabin consists of a living room/bedroom area in the front, a screened-in porch area to the side, and a kitchen to the rear. When constructing the walls, a large boulder was in his way. Not wanting to remove the boulder, Bill found a way to incorporate it into good use. While half of the boulder was on the outside of the cabin, Bill converted the inner half into kitchen shelves and the kitchen sink!

North house, 2019; photos by Thomas Crochetiere

Bill and Frances attempted to plant fruit trees in their orchard, but as the ground was very hard, the trees would not take root. Bill used an auger to dig a hole as deep as he could. He then lit a couple of sticks of dynamite and dropped them down the hole and ran like heck! As a result of the exploding dynamite, a large crater was created, allowing the newly planted trees to take root more easily. To this day, a few trees remain which were planted in 1918.

When Bill began to work and live at the Desert Queen Mill site, a five-stamp mill (machine that crushes ore) was already in place there. After Bill acquired ownership of the site, he used the stamp mill to process his ore. The mill was large and very noisy. It crushed the ore with such force, it shook the ground, much like an earthquake. With all the noise and earth shaking, Bill and Frances' babies had trouble sleeping and the chickens stopped laying eggs.

In 1924, Bill acquired a one-stamp mill from a mill site in the Gold Park Mining District (near the north entrance of present-day Joshua Tree National Park) and brought it to the ranch. The one-stamp mill replaced the use of the five-stamp mill, and operated with a lot less noise and ground shaking. This made Frances happy, as the babies now slept well and the chickens started to lay eggs again.

One-Stamp Mill, 2019;
photo by Thomas Crochetiere

Like the five-stamp mill, the one-stamp mill was powered by a steam engine. Bill later converted it to run off a gas engine. Sometime after 1948, Bill dismantled the five-stamp mill and sold it.

When other miners would give up and walk away from their claims, Bill would file a new claim on them and either work the mine or just repurpose anything they may have left behind. Bill often sold such items to new or existing miners who were in need. He would sell what mines he no longer wanted or needed or he would lease a mine to anyone who wanted to give a try to find their riches.

In 1925, Bill acquired the Hidden Gold Mine, which was located near present-day Keys View. Packing the ore out on burros down the steep face of the mountain, Bill began to build a road from the mountaintop to Hidden Valley, near his ranch. Upon the completion of the road, he named the overlook, "Keys View." The road leading to the new view was called "Keys View Road." Soon afterward, cartographers began to place that name on all the maps.

Bill Keys, circa 1930s; NPS photo

Located near present-day Hidden Valley Campground is what is known as "the iron door cave." The iron door cave is a cave with an "iron door" attached to it, and is about 120 square feet with enough room to stand up in. The origin of the cave is a mystery to many. Rumor has it that Bill Keys built it to "lock up" one of his children who had gone insane. Another story has been shared that Bill used it to stash his gold from nearby gold mines. Both could not be further from the truth.

Iron Door Cave, 2016; photos by Angela Cutts

As it turns out, Bill Keys is believed to have built it. However, it was not to lock up any of his children. As Bill was using dynamite to blast rock away at the Hidden Gold Mine, Frances did not want him to store the dynamite at the ranch. So, he built the iron door bunker around 1925/1926 so he would have a safe and secure place to keep the dynamite and pick it up on his way to the Hidden Gold Mine.

Not long after he arrived in the area, Bill Keys became friends with an old-time miner named Johnny Lang. Johnny had been prospecting in the area since 1890.

On January 25, 1926, Johnny tacked a note on his shack saying something to the effect, "Gone for grub. Be back soon." He died along the trail next to what is now known as Keys View Road. Johnny's mummified body was found two months later, on March 25th, by Bill, along with his friends Jeff Peeden and Frank Kiler. They dug a grave for Johnny and buried him on the spot.

Photo of Bill Keys with Jeff Peeden, taken by Frank Kiler

Bill spent long hours tending to livestock such as mules, burros, horses, cattle, goats, milk cows, and whatever they would need to survive. They also had chickens for eggs and meals and raised domestic rabbits. They had an amazing orchard and garden as well as crop fields. Over time, Bill had up to 30 mines at one time and worked each of them until they had nothing more to give.

Bill had a knack of thinking outside of the box. Since wood could be hard to come by, he found ways to repurpose almost anything. Needing a "tack room" to store his saddles, bridles, harnesses, and other equipment, he used two old cyanide vats! Cyanide was used to separate the gold from the ore and could be very dangerous. Bill converted these vats for a more practical use of the day. He stacked one vat on top of another, connecting them, and added a door on the side so the tack would be easy to access and kept out of the harsh weather.

By Thomas Crochetiere, 2019

Bill and Frances also had domestic dogs at the ranch to keep wild animals away. Wanting to conserve some wood, Bill took an old funnel used for large quantities of cyanide and converted it into a dog house. He cut a hole in the side to allow his dogs easy access. However, his dogs saw things differently. You see, no matter how well Bill cleaned out the funnel, it still smelled funny and this new metal dog house got very hot in the harsh desert summers. Needless to say, the dogs never used it!

By Kevin Crochetiere, 2023

As the family grew, so did the ranch and their cattle herd. They always took on temporary help in trade for room and board and had an occasional visitor at the ranch.

Johann "John" Samuelson (a Swedish immigrant) arrived at Bill Keys ranch in 1926, looking for work. Bill hired him to help with his Hidden Gold Mine as well as work around the ranch.

John and his wife Margaret took up a homestead nearby at Quail Springs. Inspired by religion, politics, nature, and solitude, it was during this time John chiseled various sayings on eight nearby flat, smooth rocks in a boulder field. After building a homestead cabin and chiseling on the nearby rocks, John filed his homestead claim. Within a year, he was notified that, since he was not a U.S. citizen, the claim would not be honored. John sold his homestead and he and Margaret moved to the Los Angeles area.

One of Samuelson's rocks, 2019; photo by Thomas Crochetiere

In 1929, John and Margaret entered a dance competition in Compton, California. As the story goes, they were one of two couples who were still competing to win. During a break, John allegedly shot and killed the other couple and announced he and Margaret were the winners. He was immediately arrested and awaited trial.

In 1930, John Samuelson was declared insane and did not stand trial. He was sent to the California State Hospital, Mendocino State Asylum for the Insane. Later that year, John escaped the hospital and fled northward. He did not take Margaret with him.

While evading his pursuers, John made his way north through Oregon and into Washington. He eventually got a job at a remote logging camp somewhere in Washington. John reportedly led a quiet life and never returned to California.

Beginning in 1940, John started to write to Bill Keys. He continued to write to him until 1954 and listed Bill as his next of kin with his employer. John wrote he wanted to return to the California desert but feared he would be arrested once he got there.

In 1954, Bill received a letter from the camp's officials informing him that John Samuelson had been hurt in a logging accident and was near death. Soon after, Bill received another letter saying he had passed away from his injuries.

Bill purchased a 1917 Fordson tractor from Phil Sullivan of Twentynine Palms in 1927. First, he used the tractor to plow the orchard and garden area. As Bill got older, cutting firewood became daunting, so he converted it to power the saw mill. This came in handy for cutting up firewood!

Fordson was a brand name of general-purpose tractors that were mass-produced starting in 1917 by Henry Ford & Sons.

Photo by Thomas Crochetiere, 2019

Every ranch needed chickens to provide eggs for meals and the chickens themselves for meat. Bill had a more unusual chicken coop than most people. His came complete with the body of an old car! It did not seem to serve any other purpose than for the pleasure of the chickens. This is more commonly known today as the "chicken coupe."

Photo by Thomas Crochetiere, 2019

One day in 1927, a lawyer named Erle Stanley Gardner stopped by the ranch for a visit. He told Bill he was inspired by the area for a book he was writing. He returned often and stayed at the ranch during several of his visits. A few years later, Erle published a series of books about a trial lawyer and detective named Perry Mason.

In the late 1920s, the Will Shay Cattle Company was Bill's biggest competitor. Every year, during the roundup, one of Shay's men (Homer Urton) would gather Bill's cattle and take them to Shay's cattle yards. Bill often attended these roundups to stop Urton from taking his cattle. This was one of many confrontations Bill had with Urton.

Bill continuously caught Urton trespassing on his ranch property. He told him not to trespass again and posted a sign along the road warning Urton to stay out. Bill thought Urton continued to trespass just to taunt him.

One day, Urton, along with a friend and two women, drove his car through Bill's ranch. When he came across the sign, he got out of his car and tore it up. Soon after Bill discovered this, he saw Urton driving towards him. Bill stopped the car, and Urton reached into his back pocket and pulled out a gun. Bill took out his rifle and fired one shot, hitting Urton in the arm. Urton fled the area and reported the shooting to the sheriff.

Later that night, the deputies came out to the ranch and arrested Bill. He quickly got out on bail and hired an attorney. A few months later, the trial began and lasted only a few days. After the trial, it was proven that Bill fired in self-defense and was acquitted. I do not believe Homer Urton ever trespassed again!

A story has been shared over the years saying that when young, the Keys kids wanted to dig their own mine to find gold and get rich. Bill thought this was a great idea and showed them where to dig. Taking turns, they began to dig, and dig they did.

After digging down several feet, they found no gold or treasure. By the end of the day, they lost interest. They said to their dad, "you were wrong this time," and started to leave. Bill told them to stop and had them help relocate the "outhouse" to a new spot at the hole they had just dug (they never made that mistake again)!

An outhouse at the ranch, 2019;
photo by Thomas Crochetiere

About every 2 weeks was laundry day. Frances used an old washboard to scrub and clean the clothes. She then wrung the water out by hand and hung the clothes on the clothesline to dry. This took a lot of time and effort to do. It was hard on her hands and was backbreaking work!

In 1929, Bill bought Frances a Model 30 Maytag wringer-washer to do their laundry. She would build a fire under a bucket of water, pour the warm water into the washing machine, and use the hand crank agitator to clean the clothes. She then ran them through the wringer and hung them on the clothesline to dry.

Photo by Thomas Crochetiere, 2019

Bill fashioned an old wagon wheel for Frances to hang her delicates, such as her stockings and

unmentionables. Bill later converted the washing machine so that it was operated by a gas engine. Frances continued to do their laundry with her Maytag washer up to her death.

Photo by Kevin Crochetiere, 2023

In 1930, Bill bought the nearby Wall Street Mill from Oran Booth and Earle McInnis. Having bought the mill just a few years earlier, they could not make a go of it. While talking with Oran, Bill learned he was a teacher. Bill asked him if he liked the desert, and

Oran told him yes. Bill asked Oran if he would be willing to come and live at the ranch and, in exchange for room and board, teach his children, Willis and Virginia.

Wall Street Mill, 2019; photo by
Thomas Crochetiere

Bill explained to Oran that this would free up Frances to run the ranch as she would like. Oran agreed and Bill built a small cabin to function as a schoolhouse. This was the first of three schoolhouses located at Desert Queen Ranch.

First schoolhouse, 2019; photo by
Thomas Crochetiere

Soon after Bill hired Oran Booth, word got out, and other families living in the area brought their children to the school at the Desert Queen Ranch. After Oran taught there for about six months, the San Bernardino County School Superintendent declared Desert Queen School an emergency school and began to pay for school supplies and the teacher's salary. Lela Carlson was hired to be the teacher, replacing Oran Booth.

By 1932, they quickly outgrew the small schoolhouse, so Bill moved school operations to the north house (above the ranch house) for a while. After Lela Carlson left, Miss Starr became the teacher in the fall of 1935.

The southern schoolhouse was built in 1935-1936. Mrs. Marsh and her husband began teaching in September 1936. Della Dudley and her husband, Rev. Howard Dudley, were the last to teach at the school; they were hired in 1937. The Desert Queen School closed in 1942 after the youngest Keys child (Phyllis; pictured in the center) left to attend school away from the ranch.

The Dudley's at the third schoolhouse; NPS photo

In 1900, C.O. Barker of Barker and Shay Cattle Company began construction of what is now Barker Dam. The dam was to catch water to allow them to increase the size of an already existing pool of water to make it a permanent watering hole to support large herds of cattle.

Barker completed his dam in 1902. However, it was determined that the location where the dam was built and the surrounding land was all public domain. His intention to file a homestead claim on the land was denied under the Forest Reserve Act of 1891. Nevertheless, Barker and Shay remained for a few years until they moved operations to Cow Camp.

Bill built a road from Hidden Valley to Barker Dam in 1921. This allowed him to haul supplies and equipment to the dam. In 1932, Bill filed a claim on the Chief Mill site, which included Barker Dam. Bill's claim was declared null and void as Barker Dam was still considered public domain, and part of the public water reserve.

The rejection of Bill's claim made him very angry, so he, his mother-in-law and Bill McHaney started to obtain homestead titles to the land surrounding the dam. Bill then began to fence the land and threatened to deny access to the dam to the public. The threat of closure caused considerable friction between Bill and other homesteaders and cattlemen; however, he would never close off access to the water. Bill disregarded their rejection and started to make further improvements to the dam.

Beginning to lose his eyesight, 74-year-old Bill McHaney moved into a cabin at Keys Desert Queen Ranch in 1933. Bill Keys set up a sort of intercom system between the cabin and ranch house to communicate with Bill. On January 5, 1937, Bill McHaney died of pneumonia in his cabin; he was 77 years old.

Bill McHaney at his cabin, circa 1936; NPS photo

Bill built the Squaw Tank Dam in 1934, along present-day Geology Tour Road. Known today as Paac Kuvuhu'k (Serrano Indian term that loosely means "place of temporary water"), it is a concrete dam located in a wash about 100 feet southeast of stop #9 of the Geology Tour Road. He built the dam as a catchment for his herd of cattle to graze and water in the Pleasant Valley area. The area has natural water catch-basins and bowl-like mortars that were hollowed into the rocks and used to grind seeds and other bits of food into meal by Indigenous people for hundreds of years.

In 1936, Bill used dynamite to blast a notch through the walls of present-day Hidden Valley Trail to improve access for his cattle. Hidden Valley had been used by cattlemen for years as a natural corral for their cattle herds.

In 1936, Bill and Frances' 10-year-old son, Ellsworth, was cranking the windlass to pull up a bucket of water from the well. The metal handle either slipped out of his hands or the brake disengaged when he thought it was latched, and the handle struck him on the head. Bill and Frances did what they could for Ellsworth, and took him to a doctor in Banning, California. The doctor soon transferred Ellsworth to a hospital in Los Angeles for treatment. After a few months in the Los Angeles hospital, he died from his injuries at age 11 and was brought home and buried in the family cemetery.

The windlass, 2019;
photo by Thomas Crochetiere

Through the tireless efforts of conservationist Minerva Hamilton Hoyt for the preservation of the California desert, Joshua Tree National Monument was established on August 10, 1936, by Presidential Proclamation under the Antiquities Act of 1906. The creation of Joshua Tree National Monument was signed into law by President Franklin D. Roosevelt. Yosemite National Park oversaw the new Joshua Tree National Monument until 1940. This new national monument completely encircled Bill Keys Desert Queen Ranch, among others.

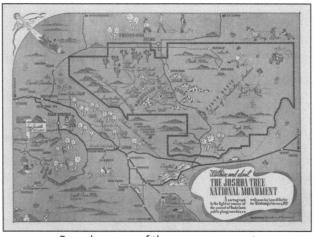

Boundary map of the new monument
as appeared in Westways Magazine, 1937;
drawn by Lowell Butler

With the creation of a new national monument, all valid privately held lands within the monument were recognized and preserved. This made the Desert Queen Ranch private property within the new monument. However, this created problems with landownership within the monument boundaries.

By order of the National Park Service (NPS) under the Taylor Grazing Act of 1934, area ranchers, cattlemen, and miners within the new monument were told they could no longer run their cattle at large without permission. This also created conflicts between current cattlemen and miners who did not want to be confined within their land only. This also limited the size of the herd Bill and other cattlemen could have.

With this new monument now being visited by so many travelers, Bill and Frances became frustrated with the many trespassers. At first, Bill put up no trespassing signs but they were ignored. It seemed that when these monument visitors saw the sign, they were curious as to what the national monument was hiding.

When they came upon the ranch house, they could not believe their eyes and wondered if anyone lived out in the middle of nowhere. When they knocked on the ranch house door, they immediately asked; why do you live here?

Frances told Bill he could not shoot them, and then she came up with an idea. She always had extra food left over from canning season, and she had a large collection of trinkets and treasures she collected from the area, so she decided to see if any of these unwanted visitors were hungry and asked if they would like to buy some food and/or "monument" souvenirs.

This worked out so well that she asked Bill to build her a separate building to display and store her goods. In the early 1940s, Bill began construction on what is known today as the "storehouse and museum."

Storehouse, 2019;
photo by Thomas Crochetiere

When Bill filed on abandoned claims, he would repurpose everything he could, and this included the cabins. He would disassemble the cabins, bring them to where he wanted them, and reassemble them. In 1937-1938, Bill assembled one of the cabins at his ranch, using it as a "guesthouse." It was also used as a cabin monument visitors could rent if they wanted to stay in the area for a night or two.

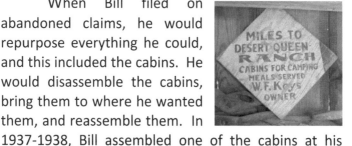

Guesthouse, 2019;
photo by Thomas Crochetiere

Not only would Bill offer monument visitors the use of the guesthouse, but he would also "rent" beds for those who wanted to sleep under the stars! Guests who stayed in the cabin or slept under the

stars were also offered breakfast in the morning (bed and breakfast, as it were). Sleeping under the stars became quite popular.

Rental beds, 2019;
photo by Thomas Crochetiere

In 1941, Bill built a unique vehicle that was a cross between a truck and an Iowa farm wagon. With daughters Patricia and Phyllis tagging along, Bill drove this custom vehicle in the annual Cherry Festival Parade in Beaumont, California. They also drove it in the Pioneer May Day Festival Parade in Twentynine Palms. The event continues to this day and is now known as Pioneer Days.

Bill's custom-made truck, circa 1941;
NPS photo

By the 1930s, Bill and Frances expanded the family gardens. Fruits and vegetables from the garden and orchard were canned in amounts to provide the whole family with food for the entire winter. Bill fertilized the soil with manure from horses, cattle, and mules.

Bill and Frances built three dams above the ranch house and orchard in the 1920s to protect it from flash floods. During the monsoonal rains of the summer, it could rain hard for an hour or more, causing the water to come over the dams. Often, the overflow was several feet high, endangering the orchard and house. Around 1940, Bill began to build a retaining wall along the wash to protect the orchard and house.

Bill made his blocks by hand, using a hand crank drill, a hammer, wedges, and a chisel. He drilled holes every 3 to 4 inches in a straight line in boulders where he wanted to break the rock. Bill would then hammer steel wedges along the line to eventually break the rock apart, creating blocks.

Drill and tongs, 2019; photos by Thomas Crochetiere

Bill often hired people to help around the ranch. He always appreciated an extra pair of helping hands. By 1943, the wall was nearly complete. However, work stopped while he was serving time in prison. He was able to complete it soon after his return home.

In 1951, Bill then began to build a retaining wall by the house. He was concerned if the north dam failed for any reason, the flood could destroy the house.

Bill used the same process to create the blocks he needed. He could not, however, lift them over his head. He used a crane boom with a tackle system and heavy-duty tongs to lift the heavy blocks into place to construct the wall. This wall was a slow process, but he finally completed the work in 1958. In the end, Bill created hundreds and hundreds of these blocks by hand!

Wall protecting the house, 2019; photo by Thomas Crochetiere

From all his hard work, Bill suffered from back trouble which gave him a lot of problems. He built a traction bench where he would lie down on his back, raising his arms above his head and had his kids attach the rope to his feet, cranked the winch, and pulled his spine into alignment. Bill would lie there for about 30 minutes to an hour to get some relief (in a way, a self-taught chiropractor).

Winch and traction bench, 2019; photos by Thomas Crochetiere

I do not know if this is true, but I believe the kids would occasionally say to each other, "you know, the old man was kind of hard on us today," and gave the winch a couple of extra cranks!

In January 1942, World War II was in full swing, and the U.S. government asked all beef producers to step up their production for the war effort. Bill soon began negotiations with the park service for grazing rights. In addition to Bill's application, his newest competitor in the area was Jim Stocker, who also applied. Stocker had a cattle ranch at the nearby Warren's Well in present-day Yucca Valley, California.

It did not help that Stocker was the Undersheriff for the San Bernardino County Sheriff's Office and oversaw their Twentynine Palms office. Bill did not think he had a chance to get the rights to enlarge his herd and graze on park service lands. He felt the sheriff's office would have an unfair influence on the park service over him.

After nearly a year and a half of negotiations for grazing rights, Bill received the first opportunity to graze his cattle within the monument in early 1943 over Stocker. However, this would not last long, as Bill would lose his grazing rights to Stocker over an unfortunate incident involving Bill and a neighbor that would soon happen. Stocker went on to become Sheriff of San Bernardino County in 1946.

In 1942, Bill met General George S. Patton. Patton established the Desert Training Center (DTC) in early 1942 and stationed troops throughout the Mojave Desert. The Mojave was a wasteland that had easy access to the railroad and seemed to General Patton to be an excellent place to train troops during World War II.

Camp Young and Camp Coxcomb were established next to Joshua Tree National Monument. Camp Young was the headquarters of the DTC and was located just south of present-day Joshua Tree National Park. Bill often visited the camps and told stories to the young and impressionable troops.

Bill later acquired a Servel gas (propane) refrigerator and a propane stove from one of Patton's

nearby DTC camps. The camp had been abandoned when the troops set out for North Africa. Bill is believed to have filed a claim on the land in 1943 and brought the appliances home. Frances continued to use the wood-burning stove in the winter to help heat the house.

By Thomas Crochetiere, 2023

Like all rural cabins, the ranch had one or more outhouses to do their business. To bathe, they heated water at the fireplace and took sponge baths. Sometime in the mid to late 1930s, Bill acquired a bathroom from the El Dorado Mine in the nearby Pinyon Mining District and moved it to the ranch. It came complete with an old-fashioned style bathtub

and water heater. For years, the new bathroom was set up in the west yard where they took hot showers. It was not until the 1950s that Bill finally attached the bathroom to the back of the ranch house. Frances was happy she now had an indoor bathing room!

By Thomas Crochetiere, 2023

A man by the name of Worth Bagley (a former deputy sheriff from Los Angeles), bought some land in 1936 between Desert Queen Ranch and Wall Street Mill. A portion of the road leading up to the mill crossed Bagley's land. Bagley (who *was not* related to the Bagley family in Twentynine Palms) told Bill to stop trespassing on his property by driving on the road to Wall Street Mill.

Bill knew he had the legal right to drive on the pre-existing road that had been there for many years. Bagley went as far as to complain about the amount of water Bill and Frances drew from their water wells. He said it was draining water from his well. Bill ignored Bagley's complaints, but they were never-ending. Bill often saw Bagley standing on the hill overlooking the road and wondered what he might be up to.

On May 11, 1943, while Bill was working all day at the Wall Street Mill, Bagley put up a sign on the road that read, "KEYS, THIS IS MY LAST WARNING, STAY OFF MY PROPERTY." As Bill was returning home from the Wall Street Mill, he came across the sign and stopped to check it out. A short time later, Bill saw Bagley walking up the road towards him with a gun in his hand. As Bill turned back towards his car, Bagley opened fire with his gun and started to shoot at him. Bagley missed Bill but did shoot his car at least once. Bill then got his gun from the car and shot back, killing Bagley where he stood.

Later that day, Bill turned himself in to the deputy in Twentynine Palms. The deputy did not believe it was self-defense, and Bill was arrested and charged with murder. Frances sold their remaining cattle, took all their savings out of the bank, and mortgaged the ranch to hire an attorney for Bill. At the age of 63, Bill Keys was convicted of manslaughter and sentenced to 10 years in San Quentin State Prison.

Soon after Bill was sent to prison, the National Park Service changed the name of Keys View to Salton View. By NPS policy, a location within a national monument cannot be named after a living person. The road Bill built going up to the view was subsequently changed to Salton View Road.

By this time, Bill and Frances' youngest daughters, Patricia, and Phyllis, were attending high school in Alhambra, California. Frances moved there and rented a house for her, Willis, Patricia, and Phyllis to live in.

Willis had been working at a defense plant in Alhambra since 1939, and Virginia joined the Navy in 1942 and was deployed. Frances too got a job at a defense plant while Bill was in prison. Being so far away from the ranch often worried Frances, so she, Patricia, and Phyllis returned to the ranch permanently in 1944.

This was hard on Frances and she tried everything she could think of to get Bill released from prison. Then, in 1948, she remembered Bill's lawyer friend Erle Stanley Gardner and wrote to him. Erle wrote back saying he remembered his friend Bill, and agreed to look into his case.

During an interview with Worth Bagley's last wife (his ninth wife), she told Gardner that Bagley was obsessed with killing Bill Keys. She said Bagley was trying to find ways to kill Bill and get away with it. She told him this was well documented in the divorce papers she filed with the court. When Gardner asked her if she shared this information with the deputy who interviewed her, she said yes, but he must have forgotten to mention that during the trial. With this new information in hand, Gardner had what he needed to get Bill Keys out of prison.

Erle Stanley Gardner presented this new evidence at Bill's parole hearing. With Frances never giving up on Bill and with the help of his friend Erle, he accepted early release and immediate parole from San Quentin Prison on October 25, 1948. The parole board told Bill they believed he was wrongly convicted and although they could not overturn the court's conviction, they would refer his case to the governor's advisory board for consideration of a pardon.

At age 69, Bill Keys was released from San Quentin. While in prison, Bill did not openly harbor a grudge and considered his years there his college years. He furthered his education and tried his hand at creating paintings.

In 1945, Erle Stanly Gardner was contacted by a California public defender who was overwhelmed by a case he needed help with. The public defender had a client he believed was innocent but he could not prove it. Gardner offered to help and got their client acquitted. Gardner took on other similar cases as well as Bill's case in 1948. With his intervention in these cases, it sparked an innocence project of the day called the "Court of Last Resort," which was featured in a monthly column of a magazine starting in September 1948.

Later, on July 12, 1956, the governor's advisory board ruled against the courts' conviction of Bill Keys, and he was granted an unconditional (full) pardon from Governor Goodwin Knight of California.

Throughout their time away, Frances' brother, Aaron, would occasionally stay at the ranch to keep things in working order. However, during their absence, the ranch house had been broken into, and the ranch property was vandalized several times. This is what prompted Frances to return to the ranch.

While Bill was in prison, their daughters Patricia and Phyllis both graduated high school. Patricia got married, living nearby in Joshua Tree, and Phyllis came home to live for a while. Their son Willis joined the Army in 1945 and their daughter Virginia finished her tour in the Navy and got married. Willis' tour in the Army ended around the time his father was released from prison. He returned home for a while to help his father.

When Bill got home from prison, he kept himself busy by making a lot of repairs around the ranch. One of the first things he did was carve out a stone monument and placed it where he was ambushed by Worth Bagley.

Bill wrote on the monument saying, "Here is where Worth Bagley bit the dust at the hand of W.F. Keys May 11, 1943." A metal replica of the original monument still stands today along the Wall Street Mill Trail in present-day Joshua Tree National Park.

Worth Bagley monument, 2019;
photo by Thomas Crochetiere

Not long after Bill returned from prison, he came across a 1922 Mack truck stuck in the sand near the town of Joshua Tree. It was being used to construct a new road from Joshua Tree to the present-day west entrance of the monument.

Frances told Bill it had been stuck in the sand for several months and she had not seen anyone attempt to get it out. The truck was believed to have belonged to the County of San Bernardino, which seemed to have abandoned it.

Finding the truck still there, Bill got it out of the sand and brought it to the ranch. As far as he was concerned, they no longer wanted it and he did (finders, keepers).

1922 Mack truck, 2019; photo by Thomas Crochetiere

Mack Trucks was founded in 1900 by Jack and Gus Mack in Brooklyn, NY, and was originally known as the Mack Brothers Company.

As the Mack truck has been a fixture of Keys Desert Queen Ranch, it had been parked at the ranch and not moved from 1969 to 2005. One day, when a park ranger arrived to give a ranch tour, he noticed the Mack truck was no longer parked in its regular spot.

At first, it was a great mystery how this might have occurred. It had been parked in the same spot since 1969. How did it get moved? Who moved it and why?

In October 2005, during one of Willis' many visits to the ranch, he told one of the park rangers he bet the Mack truck could still run. She told him she did not believe it could, as it had not been driven for many years. Willis said he was sure it could, and she told him to give it a try. Seeing what parts he needed, Willis returned the next day. He replaced the battery and spark plugs, drained the fuel, and replaced it, started it up and took it for a joyride around the ranch!

One day in late 1948, a doctor from Los Angeles stopped by the ranch and wanted to buy a mining claim from Bill. Bill admired the Willys Jeep the doctor was driving and offered to trade a mining claim for the Jeep.

Willys Jeep, 2019; photo by Thomas Crochetiere

After the deal was struck, the Jeep became Bill's favorite vehicle.  It is a one-quarter ton, four-wheel drive, and could go anyplace he would ever want to go.

Originally, the Jeep had a canvas top that wore out regularly.  In 1956, Willis took the Jeep to his brother-in-law's shop in Joshua Tree where he cut up an old Ford Model A, fitting its roof as a hard top for the Jeep.

The Jeep legend began in November 1940, in the early days of World War II, a year before the United States entered the war. Willys Overland Motors, Inc./Jeep began in Toledo, OH.

In 1948, a road was constructed by the National Park Service from the west entrance to Hidden Valley (present-day Park Blvd).  This new road passed near Bill's ranch.  With dreams of transforming his ranch into a dude ranch and resort, Bill carved out a road from the present-day Boy Scout Trail/Keys West Backcountry Trailhead along the new road to his ranch as a shortcut.

To attract more visitors to his ranch, Bill created the Boy Scout Trail in the 1950s, connecting his new ranch road to Indian Cove Campground to the north.  While the Boy Scouts were camping at Indian Cove, he hoped they would use this new trail as a reason to visit.

Some years had more rain than others. The ranch dams were often full, and Bill called it Keys Lake. Bill would also stock it with fish from time to time. The biggest snowfall on record in the area occurred in January 1949. During this snowstorm, the lake had about 2 feet thick of ice. Bill fashioned a pair of ice skates for people to wear to ice skate on the frozen lake.

Beginning in 1949, Bill raised Barker Dam three feet with concrete forms and built another retaining dam below the larger one. He completed his work in 1950 with the inscription "Bighorn Dam, Built by Willis Keys & Wm. F. Keys – Phyllis Ann Keys – F.M. Keys, 1949-50." Bill called it the Bighorn Dam due to the many bighorn sheep that were coming to the area for water. The dam still stands today.

Barker Dam with three-foot extension, circa 2010;
NPS photo

By the mid-1950s, Joshua Tree National Monument was being visited by filmmakers, Marines from a base in Twentynine Palms, Boy Scouts, and many others. In 1959, Hollywood paid a visit to Bill Keys. They wanted to use his Desert Queen Ranch as a staging location to film one of their movies. They were so impressed with Bill, they offered him a starring role in their movie. "Wild Burro of the West," is an episode of The Wonderful World of Disney that first aired on January 29, 1960. It was filmed in Joshua Tree National Monument and Bill Keys played the role of a prospector in it.

Wild Burro of the West, 1960;
courtesy of The Walt Disney Studios

Bill drove his 1922 Mack truck in the movie. The truck routinely overheated and did not have a radiator cap. To make due until he got a cap, Bill used a "potato" in place of the missing radiator cap. Now, when it overheated, the potato would pop out and lunch was served!

"Chico, the Misunderstood Coyote," an episode of Walt Disney's Wonderful World of Color, first aired on October 15, 1961. It was also filmed in the Joshua Tree National Monument. The Desert Queen Ranch was again used as a staging location, but Bill did not have a part in this movie.

It has been purported that during the filming of one of the two Disney movies, the Indigenous people's petroglyphs along present-day Barker Dam Trail did not stand out in the film as they hoped. So, members of the film crew painted over the top of some of the petroglyphs to improve them. However, an NPS report written in 1975 suggests the painting may have been done by a film crew as early as the 1920s in connection with a movie featuring "Hollywood" Indians. Whoever painted over the petroglyphs, we may never know.

In the late 1950s, a group of wealthy equestrians from Palm Springs, California rode up to an area later named "Piano Rock" south of Barker Dam. Barker Dam is located east of the Desert Queen Ranch. They would have all their gear sent up ahead of them, along with a chuck wagon, where their meals were prepared. This was a big event for them and was done annually. The group was led by Frank Bogert, who would become mayor of Palm Springs. On occasion, a piano was brought up and placed on a big flat rock off present-day Barker Dam Trail and played for their entertainment.

Bill had been rumored to have played the piano on Piano Rock on occasion, but his son, Willis, dispelled this. In fact, at first, Bill was angered about the loud piano and feared it would disturb the cattle. However, the piano music seemed to have the opposite effect and calmed them.

In addition to Erle Stanley Gardner, the Keys family hosted other well-known visitors, such as prominent botanists Phillip Munz and Edmund Jaeger. During one of Jaeger's visits to the ranch, he identified a new desert flower, which he named "Keysia" (Glyptopleura marginata) to honor the kindness the Keys showed to him and the many desert travelers who would visit the ranch.

As the years continued to pass, Bill and Frances started to get old together. Their children were all married and had families of their own. Sadly, on January 9, 1963, Frances passed away; she was 75.

Frances, circa 1918          Frances, circa 1955

Frances was buried in the Twentynine Palms Cemetery. Bill, being too sick at the time, was not able to protest her burial at that location. When he later recovered, Bill obtained permission from San Bernardino County to reinter her body in the family cemetery located near the ranch alongside their three children who had died many years before. Bill carved her a headstone inlaid with turquoise.

Not long after her mother's death, Patricia Keys Garry was able to track down one of her father's sisters. Patricia learned that the sister was originally from Culbertson, Nebraska, and was now residing in a retirement home in Pasadena, California. Patricia arranged for her father (age 84) to reunite with his sister Mollie Barth Townsend (age 75) after 70 years of separation. As it turned out, she had been living in Southern California for the past 20 years. Mollie passed away less than two years later at the age of 76.

Coincidentally, Bill's mother, Margaret, lived in Los Angeles with his sister, Catherine Barth Honnell, from 1924 to 1928. When Margaret passed away in 1928, she was interred in Culbertson, Nebraska, alongside her husband, John Barth (who passed away in 1917). I do not believe Bill ever knew that his sister Catherine, nor his mother, lived so close. I do not think he ever knew about his sister, Mollie, living so close until Patricia located her in 1963.

After Frances' death, Bill became very lonely around the ranch. Their children were living their own lives and had little interest in the ranch. Bill decided to recruit people to come and live at the ranch, and in exchange for room and board, they could help with the day-to-day upkeep of the ranch. With this in mind, Bill had no trouble finding young people with nothing else to do but take him up on his offer. The only problem was, these "young people" were a product of the 1960s.

This was the beginning of the so-called counterculture, where these new "guests" preferred to celebrate their personal freedom at the expense of traditional social values. Most of them rejected many of the social, economic, and political values of their parent's generation and were of absolutely no help around the ranch!

Bill decided to sell the ranch in 1964 and approached the National Park Service to buy his Desert Queen Ranch. Unfortunately, the NPS would have to plan for such a transaction to take place and budget for it. Not doing this, and not having the money in their budget, they passed on the purchase.

Not letting this stop him, Bill sold the Desert Queen Ranch to an investor, Henry "Hank" Tubman from Los Angeles, in October 1964. Bill retained ownership of the one-acre family cemetery.

Bill had only one provision. He wanted to continue living at the ranch until his death. Tubman agreed and started making plans to build a dude ranch and resort there. Bill was 85 years old at the time.

Seeing no telephone poles or electrical lines at or near the ranch, Tubman asked Bill where he got his electricity. Bill pointed to the generator and told him it was old and he might want to replace it. Bill shared that they have been using kerosene lamps for their lighting since they have been living there. Tubman also saw no fire hydrants and asked Bill where he got his water. Bill showed him the ranch wells and told him they were running dry and they would need to be dug down deeper. Bill also told him they had no telephone service at the ranch. Tubman told Bill this was not a problem, as he had financial backing and told him that money could buy anything.

Tubman soon approached the county to have the utilities brought to the ranch. The county quickly told him, since the ranch was surrounded by a national park, he would need to go through them. When Tubman contacted the park service, they told him it would not happen. They explained that their primary responsibility was to preserve and protect the scenic, natural, and cultural resources of the national monument, and allowing utilities to be installed would be in direct contradiction with their policy.

By 1966, Tubman was unable to secure the necessary permits or get the needed utilities. His financial backing also started to fade away. He soon abandoned his plans and began negotiations with the park service to sell the ranch to them.

On October 28, 1966, Hank Tubman traded Keys Desert Queen Ranch, all 879 acres, to the NPS for land in San Diego, California. The land Tubman received in the trade is land that would become part of the Qualcomm Stadium project.

In 1967, Bill was honored by being selected to be the Grand Marshall for the Joshua Tree Turtle Days Parade. He was also a judge of the "Turtle Races," which was the main event for the weekend celebration. The turtle [tortoise] race continued for several years; however, it was discontinued in 1975. The desert tortoise was federally listed as a threatened species on April 2, 1990.

Joshua Tree Turtle Races, late 1960s; courtesy of the
Morongo Basin Historical Museum

Bill's age was finally catching up with him. He could not do what he once did and now used canes to steady his walk.

In June 1969, Bill had fallen ill. According to one of his friends, he ate very little besides baked beans, which caused an intestinal blockage. Bill was taken to the Hi-Desert Memorial Hospital in Yucca Valley (now closed), where he died on June 28, 1969, three months shy of his 90th birthday.

Bill was also buried in the family cemetery near his ranch alongside Frances and their three sons. About 150 friends and family attended his funeral. Willis Keys later carved his father's headstone and placed it on his grave on Easter Sunday in March 1978.

Bill, circa 1918          Bill, circa 1955

Sometime after his death and in memory of Bill Keys, the National Park Service changed the name of Salton View back to Keys View. They also changed the name of Salton View Road to Keys View Road.

From Keys View, you can see the San Andreas Fault, Mt. San Jacinto, and Mt. San Gorgonio. In the distance, you can view the Salton Sea, and you might be able to see Signal Mountain in Mexico.

The Keys family knew the importance of working together as a team. Bill and Frances kept medical journals at their ranch to treat any minor illness or injury they would encounter. In their orchard, they grew various fruits and vegetables. They also grew grass hay and alfalfa hay to feed their milk cows, horses, and mules. As towns began to develop nearer their ranch, they traded and negotiated with area homesteaders and businesses in Twentynine Palms and later in the communities of Yucca Valley and Joshua Tree for everyday items such as salt, coffee, sugar, flour, cereal, and spices.

Life in the desert presented many challenges. Winters could be long and cold. Summers were extreme and there would be several years with little or no rainfall. Crops would fail and water wells run dry. The work was hard and neighbors were far away.

Few homesteaders met the challenge. Many farms and small homesteads were abandoned, leaving behind the tiny cabins which still litter the desert in places today. Food and supplies were difficult to come by. At first, the closest town, Banning, was 60 miles away. They had to travel two days on a rough, deeply rutted dirt road to get there. You had to make sure you had enough food, water, and spare parts to complete the journey. This was not the life for the weak at heart. One family that not only survived but thrived in the desert was that of Bill and Frances Keys.

Spending over 44 years together, Bill and Frances made a life and raised their children in this remote desert location. Through their hard work, they built one of the largest, most self-sustaining ranches of its kind in the area.

Bill and Frances Keys, 1955; NPS photo

Excluding his time in prison, Bill Keys spent nearly 60 years of his life in and around his Desert Queen Ranch. He succeeded in the desert, and through his resourcefulness, Bill adapted to the ever-changing challenges he encountered every day. When the odds were against him, Bill never gave up. In good times and bad, Bill always had the support of his family and friends. Bill was self-taught, had to be self-reliant, and adamantly protected the needs and interests of his family, even if it came at the expense of other cattlemen and homesteaders.

This attitude sometimes caused him to be at odds with the people around him, especially when Joshua Tree National Monument was first established in 1936. Even though Bill could be difficult to work with at times, many of the surrounding homesteaders and miners considered Keys Desert Queen Ranch as the center of their desert network and thought of Bill and Frances Keys as their friends.

For income, Bill and Frances would barter to create some transactions. Bill earned money from cattle ranching, mining, and milling ore. He would hire out his ore work by the ton at both the Wall Street Mill and the mill he set up at the ranch. He did assay work and assisted other prospectors. They would sell their excess fruits and vegetables to a market in Twentynine Palms, and later in Yucca Valley and Joshua Tree.

While the world outside the ranch changed dramatically, the Keys' way of life remained remarkably constant. Bill hoped to one day turn their ranch into a recreation resort. He wanted to create small lakes along the seasonal creek near the ranch house and provide camping and a picnic area for Boy Scouts and other youth groups, civic groups, and clubs to use. Sadly, this would never be.

The historic Desert Queen Ranch was declared a Point of Historical Interest by San Bernardino County in 1974. On October 30, 1975, Keys Desert Queen Ranch was added to the National Register of Historic Places. In 1976, the National Park Service began giving guided tours to the public of Desert Queen Ranch (more commonly known today as Keys Ranch) to commemorate the nation's bicentennial.

Located in the heart of Joshua Tree National Park, Keys Ranch is a well-preserved homestead. The ranch is located at the southernmost edge of the Mojave Desert, in an area of the park known as the Wonderland of Rocks. It is closed to public access and is only accessible by reservation via a half-mile-long, 90-minute ranger-guided tour.

Bill Keys and the Desert Queen Ranch are a cornerstone of Joshua Tree National Park.

Bill at the front door of his ranch house, late 1950s;
NPS photo

# Frances Lawton Keys

Frances May Lawton was born in 1887 in Toledo (Lucas County), Ohio to parents Wallace Rathburn Lawton and Lena Hortense Weeks Lawton. Her father's work soon took the family to Ontario, Canada, and after a few years, they moved to California. After meeting and marrying Bill Keys in 1918, she would leave the comforts of the city to move to the Mojave Desert to start a family.

Frances moved into the cabin Bill had built in a remote section of the desert. Once there, she made many improvements, wallpapering and whitewashing the walls to make them look more presentable. Frances would eventually make this small cabin into a home. Although Bill promised to build her a much grander home there one day, he never did. In the end, I do not think she minded much.

Family life at the Desert Queen Ranch was hard work. Together, Frances and Bill tackled the hardships of isolated desert life. They kept many medical journals, making Frances the family doctor. She tended the livestock and worked in the family orchard almost daily. She was the school teacher to Willis and Virginia until they were 9 and 7 respectively. It was not until Bill hired a teacher that Frances was freed to run the ranch as she would like.

The family raised goats, chickens, rabbits, and cattle, and grew a wide variety of vegetables, including radishes, cucumbers, tomatoes, pumpkins, squash, corn, and beans. The children were well-versed in the daily chores of collecting eggs, milking the goats, and helping around the ranch. In their free time, they roamed the vast desert and explored as far as the eye could see. Frances made harvests last through the winter with extensive canning and preserving. She butchered animals for meat, and she cooked all the family meals on a wood-burning stove. Frances would not have the luxury of a propane stove and refrigerator until the early 1940s.

Frances was an excellent cook, cooking from memory, and did not rely on recipes. If beef was not available, she would use chicken, domestic rabbit, cottontail, or jackrabbits. Frances always made sure there was plenty to eat for breakfast and dinner. She not only fed her family; she also fed the ranch hands and guests. Frances was very creative and knew how to make things last.

Though the Desert Queen Ranch was at first far removed from any existing towns, Frances easily made friends when Twentynine Palms started to grow in the 1920s and 1930s. She sold surplus canned goods, produce, and her sunbonnets at the market in Twentynine Palms. Frances later sold these items in Yucca Valley and Joshua Tree also.

Frances had a hobby of collecting artifacts found around the old gold mines and mill sites, especially any colored glass, such as pharmacy or tobacco bottles, which she displayed at home. After the establishment of Joshua Tree National Monument, she sold many of these items to the monument visitors who came knocking on her door. She proudly displayed these items in her storehouse and museum located next to the ranch house.

When Bill was in San Quentin State Prison, Frances continued to provide for and protect the family. She did it all; mining, cattle ranching, butchering, gardening, canning, sewing, laundry, and teaching.

Frances was a wife, mother, and pioneer. She was also a force to be reckoned with. Frances did what needed to be done and was a fierce protector of her family and property. Frances Keys had great integrity and was well respected. She was a friend to many and an enemy to none.

Frances Lawton Keys, circa 1950; NPS photo

Frances at age 13; NPS photo

Bill and Frances in the snow, early 1940s;
NPS photo

Bill and Frances, Christmas in their living room, 1950;
NPS photo

Bill and Frances in their kitchen, 1955;
NPS photo

Bill and Frances in front of her display table, late 1950s;
NPS photo

Bill standing along the Joshua tree log fence in front
of the ranch house, late 1950s; NPS photo

Bill posing for a reenactment photo of the ambush by Worth Bagley, early 1960s; NPS photo

Illustration of Keys Ranch by Wayne Baczkowski;
courtesy of the Joshua Tree National Park Association

# Keys Ranch

Keys Desert Queen Ranch is in a remote, rocky canyon of Joshua Tree National Park. The area was first occupied by seasonal Indigenous people. The Serrano and Cahuilla Indians are believed to have inhabited this area as early as the 1500s to the 1800s. During the Chemehuevi-Mohave Indians War (1867-1871) in the Colorado River region, many Chemehuevi moved westward and settled in the area in 1867. The Mohave and other Indigenous people also frequented the area but did not settle. Little evidence of their presence can be found at Keys Ranch today.

Later, cattlemen arrived to graze and water their cattle while establishing a camp there. Once gold was discovered, the area was transformed into a mill site.

Bill McHaney and his brother Jim McHaney grazed Texas Longhorn cattle in the Hidden Valley area of present-day Joshua Tree National Park. Around 1888, they started the development of a camp. Their camp consisted of two adobe cabins; one was used as a bunkhouse and the other as a cookhouse. Bill McHaney befriended several of the Indigenous people in the area and worked with many of them. In 1894, they built an adobe barn. Their camp came to be known as the "McHaney Camp."

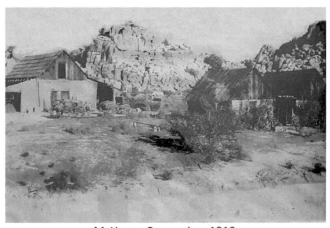

McHaney Camp, circa 1910;
courtesy of the Morongo Basin Historical Museum

In 1894, The McHaney brothers acquired ownership of the nearby Desert Queen Mine. At first, Bill and Jim McHaney hauled their ore to the Pinyon Well Mill site several miles to the south for processing. They then received financing from a bank in Los Angeles to purchase and install a five-stamp mill by Baker Ironworks of Los Angeles at the McHaney Camp. They sold off all their cattle and transformed the camp into a mill site.

The initial gold found at the Desert Queen Mine was extremely rich, but the wealth was spent as soon as it was produced. Taking this opportunity for self-indulgence, Jim McHaney spent his share on fast women and cheap booze. With the high costs of mining and milling in the desert, he quickly exhausted all available funds. To help cover costs, the brothers took out a new loan from a bank in San Bernardino.

The Desert Queen Mine was involved in much litigation during the last few months of 1895. The bank took possession of the mine and mill site, which were then sold. After changing ownership several times, William Morgan purchased both the Desert Queen Mine and Desert Queen Mill in 1907.

Bill Keys arrived in the area in 1910, at the age of 30. Bill began work as a muleskinner for the Desert Queen Mine and started living at the camp and mill site. In 1913, Bill started to build a permanent cabin to live in while staying at the camp site.

In 1917, after the death of William Morgan in 1915, the mine and mill site were deeded over to him for wages back owed to him. Bill then called the mill site "Desert Queen Ranch."

The ranch cabin was completed in 1917. First, it consisted of two rooms; a lower story room and a second-story room.

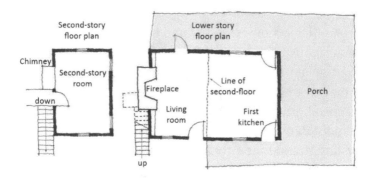

After Bill married Frances, she asked him to add a bedroom for them. He extended the lower story room to do so. Frances' mother used the second-story room when she visited. Bill cut a small hole in the ceiling above the fireplace and built a trap door to allow heat to rise into the second-story room during the cold winter months.

In 1919, Bill added a detached kitchen in front of the cabin (commonly known as a summer kitchen). In 1923, he added a bedroom off the back, under the second story, for the children. As they had more children, Bill added another much larger bedroom off the back of the cabin, transforming the first bedroom into a storage room.

In 1934, Bill removed the detached kitchen and added a much larger kitchen to the cabin (this one was attached to the front of the cabin). As years passed, he added an attached bathroom to the back of the cabin and another storage room (it is what you might call a "built more").

Their homestead would eventually include the ranch house, a store, two school houses, a cabin for the teacher to live in, a guesthouse, storage buildings, a machine shop, outhouses, a stamp mill, an arrastra, a corral, a supply yard, an orchard, water wells, cement dams, a seasonal lake, a windmill, an irrigation system, hand-made rock retaining walls, and a family cemetery.

The National Park Service (NPS) began giving guided tours of the Desert Queen Ranch in November 1975. The first public tours began in 1976, commemorating the nation's bicentennial. Tours are seasonal and are typically held from late fall to early spring. They are generally not available during the hot summer months.

Cover of the original ranch tour guide from 1976;
written and illustrated by Reino and Wendy Clark.
Courtesy of the NPS

Keys Ranch is a protected historic site. To preserve its historical character, admission to the ranch is restricted to guided walking tours. Sadly, theft and vandalism have occurred at the ranch in the past, as well as other locations within the park.

Photo by Thomas Crochetiere, 2019

Seasonal caretakers (park volunteers) live at the ranch to help keep an eye on it. They provide their own RV to live in, while the park provides them with potable water and sewage disposal. There is no electricity throughout most of the park, including the ranch. Caretakers must have their own solar/battery system and generator to provide any electricity they may need.

To learn more about Keys Ranch and the detailed history behind it, check out "Keys Desert Queen Ranch: A Visual & Historical Tour" by Thomas Crochetiere.

**Keys Ranch Tour** is .5 miles (.8 km) of walking and lasts about 90 minutes. The ranger-guided tour of the historic Keys Desert Queen Ranch includes the colorful story of the many years Bill and Frances spent working together to make a life and raise their children in this remote location.

Photo by Thomas Crochetiere, 2019

*For reservations*; visit the park website, https://www.nps.gov/jotr for the tour schedule and how to reserve your tickets.

Keys Ranch, 2019; photo by Thomas Crochetiere

**Visiting Keys Ranch is restricted to ranger led tours only. Unauthorized access without a ranger may result in arrest and/or fines.**

# Bill Keys' Birthplace

Where Bill Keys was born has been under debate for many years. Some believe he was born in Russia, while others believe he was born in Nebraska, USA. Records indicate that Bill's father, John Jacob Barth, was born in Kolb (Saratov Province), Russia in 1848 and his mother, Margaret Katherine Eckhart Barth, was born in Messer (Saratov Province), Russia, on May 1, 1850. Records show that John Jacob Barth and Margaret K. Eckhart were married in Russia in 1871.

Records also show that Bill's uncle, Jacob Barth, was a German colonist born in Kolb, Russia, on May 6, 1856. Jacob Barth, along with a brother (unknown name), and their mother, Katherine Elisabeth Barth, left Russia to go to Germany and immigrated to the United States in 1876. After arriving in Virginia in 1876, they moved to Nebraska in about 1878, eventually settling in Palisade, Nebraska. They did not stay in Palisade very long before permanently settling in nearby Culbertson, Nebraska.

Records have been found about John Jacob Barth and Jacob Barth in and around Culbertson, Nebraska. Both are interred in Culbertson. No records have been found of them having a brother. Their mother, Katherine Barth, and sister, Christina Barth Frick, are also interred in Culbertson, Nebraska.

Obituary records in 1928 of Bill's mother, Margaret, show she was born in Russia, and that they immigrated to the United States in 1892. Her obituary also stated she had thirteen children. According to obituary records in 1965 of Bill's sister, Mollie Barth Townsend, their family was from Germany, and she was born in Germany, on November 12, 1888, implying that Bill was also born in Germany or perhaps Russia. However, Bill's obituary in 1969 indicates he was born in Palisade, Nebraska.

To further complicate things, his sister, Mollie, had said she thought Bill did not run away from home until 1898, and that he was 15 years old at the time. That would have made his year of birth 1884, instead of 1879.

If so, Bill would have had to change his age to 18 to make him old enough to join Teddy Roosevelt's Rough Riders, which would make him change from the year he was born to 1879. Having changed his name along the way, his name, and the year in which he was born were now part of his enlistment records and have never changed.

Bill has maintained that he was 15 when he left home and that he left in 1894. Whether Mollie was 5 years old or 10 when Bill left home in Culbertson, Nebraska, we may never know. Having found no record of birth for Bill, I cannot confirm or deny his year of birth or place of birth.

Since we know that Bill easily changed his name after leaving home, it is equally possible he could have changed his year of birth in his attempt to enlist in Teddy Roosevelt's Rough Riders. That was common practice for many who joined the opposing armies during the American Civil War years earlier.

We do know that Bill Keys filed many homestead claims which indicated he was born in Nebraska and was a U.S.-born citizen. No records have been found of him applying for or becoming a naturalized citizen. There have never been any reports of Bill speaking with a German or Russian accent. No immigration holds were ever placed on Bill during the few times he had been arrested and jailed, or while in prison. Bill had indicated he was born in Nebraska in the U.S. census reports from 1920 to 1950. However, he said he was born in Virginia on his marriage license and certificate to Frances in 1918 and on the birth certificate of William Jr. in 1919. He said he was born in Sidney, Nebraska on Ellsworth's death certificate in 1937.

In the 1910 census report, Bill's father, John Barth, listed that he was of Russo-German descent, born in Russia. He stated he and his wife, Katherine, immigrated to the U.S. in 1892 and that his occupation was shoemaker, owning his shop. He further stated that their primary language was German.

Since Mollie stated she was born in Germany, it is possible that once the family left Russia, they temporarily migrated to Germany before her birth in 1888. Records also show that Bill and Mollie had a brother, Paul Barth, who was born in Culbertson, Nebraska in September 1892.

Given the fact that Bill's parents both stated they did not immigrate to the U.S. until 1892, it is possible, and highly probable, that Bill did not want this fact to be known. If that is the case, it would have been ingenious of him to attempt to join Teddy Roosevelt's Rough Riders in 1898, to have his place of birth and date of birth listed on an official U.S. government document. It would also have been ingenious of him to register for the World War I draft at the age of 38, given the fact, that at that age, he would never have been drafted otherwise. This act further makes his age and birthplace official on U.S. government records.

When Bill's uncle, Jacob Barth, immigrated to the U.S. in 1876, "a brother" was listed as accompanying him. Having found no records of such a brother, and having found no immigration records for their sister, Christina Barth, it is possible that the brother listed was possibly Christina. Immigration entry records from Virginia during that period are either non-existent or hard to come by. Record-keeping was much improved when Ellis Island Immigration Station opened in New York Harbor, in 1892.

We know that John Samuelson was not able to keep the land he homesteaded because he was not a U.S. citizen. Given the fact that Bill Keys had official U.S. government documents stating that he was a U.S. citizen, he had no trouble filling the many homestead claims in and near his Desert Queen Ranch.

Imagine if Bill Keys was not believed to be a U.S. citizen or had not been able to file homestead claims within present-day Joshua Tree National Park, much of the parks' history would not be as we know it today. It would bring a whole new meaning to "what if."

In an interview with Bill's son, Willis, he said his father was born in Nebraska. However, in another interview with Bill's daughter, Patricia, she said she thought he was born in Russia.

Given the fact that Bill had predominantly maintained that he was born in Nebraska, not Russia or Germany, and out of respect for him, I list his place of birth as Nebraska.

Whether Bill Keys was born in the U.S. or not, whether he was 15 or 18 years old when he left home, we may never know. What we do know is what happened from the time he left home in Culbertson, Nebraska, to his death is Bill Keys' story.

Last known photo of Bill Keys, taken December 15, 1968, by Steve Shinn Photography; NPS photo

# About the Author

Thomas Crochetiere works with the National Park Service at Joshua Tree National Park as an Interpretation-Visitor Service Representative. After retiring from a career in public service, he began working with the NPS in 2013. From the more than 302,000 eligible volunteers, Thomas was recognized for his contributions to the park service during the NPS National Volunteer Week in April 2019 and featured in an article titled "NPS Meet Our Volunteers: Tom Crochetiere." In February 2024, after volunteering more than 5,000 hours at JTNP, he was honored by being presented with the President's "Lifetime Achievement Award."

Thomas also volunteers at the California Welcome Center in Yucca Valley as a Welcome Ambassador. He is a member of the Morongo Basin Historical Museum and the Twentynine Palms Historical Society.

As a local historian, Thomas spends countless hours researching area history. While identifying and promoting historical records, he enjoys putting together the pieces of the puzzle to offer a unique perspective on events that helped shape the communities and places around us.

By Sandra Crochetiere

"As part of my job with Joshua Tree National Park, I give ranger-guided tours of Keys Ranch, home to Bill and Frances Keys. I truly enjoy sharing Bill and Frances' story with park visitors, but recently, a park visitor shared a story with me that I will never forget.

While giving a Keys Ranch Tour on April 20, 2023, a park visitor shared a story with me and asked if the person in her story might be Bill Keys:

In 1967, when she was 6 years old, she was camping near Keys Ranch with her family. She said an older man in a truck drove up and began to talk to her and her family. She noticed he was very old and he was eating a peach. The man told them he lived nearby and just stopped by to talk. She said the man went on to tell them stories of the area as he continued to eat his peach. She said when done eating the peach, he took out a knife and started to carve the peach seed. She said when he was done, he created a small animal on the peach seed and gave it to her. She told me they talked some more and then he drove away.

She asked me if I thought this person might have been Bill Keys. I told her that he was still alive in 1967, and had become very lonely after his wife, Frances, passed away in 1963. Stories have been shared that he liked to visit park visitors, just to talk and pass the time away. I told her I was 90% sure it was, in fact, Bill Keys who they met that day.

As we continued the ranch tour, she saw Bill Keys Willys Jeep and told me that it was the truck he was driving. She was sure of it. I told her I was now 100% sure she had met Bill Keys that day.

Along our tour, I pointed to a fruit tree in Bill and Frances Keys orchard and told her it was quite probable that it where he got his peach from. She told me I made her day. I told her; she made my day.

Fruit tree in Bill and Frances' orchard, 2019;
photo by Thomas Crochetiere

I failed to get her name, but I hope she one day reads her story in this book. No, she no longer has the peach seed."

# Joshua Tree National Park Association

Joshua Tree National Park Association works in partnership with Joshua Tree National Park to help in its achievement of programming goals in education and interpretation, along with scientific and historical research and activities.

The Joshua Tree National Park Association has been supporting programming at Joshua Tree National Park since 1962. As the park's primary non-profit partner, they operate the parks' visitor centers and gift shops that are often the first stop for visitors from around the world; offer a field institute with classes taught by experts in natural sciences, cultural history, and the arts; and raise funds via donations and their membership program.

As part of the California Desert Protection Act of 1994, Joshua Tree National Monument was elevated to National Park status on October 31, 1994.

This book, and others in the JTNP series, are available at park visitor centers and gift shops as well as the JTNPA online book store, **www.joshuatree.org.**

# Notes

_____

_____

_____

_____

_____

_____

_____

_____

_____

_____

_____

_____

_____

_____